The Sunflower and the Sun

Chloe Dow

BookLeaf
Publishing

India | USA | UK

Presentation by *BookLeaf Publishing*

Web: www.bookleafpub.com

E-mail: info@bookleafpub.com

ISBN : 9789357447072

First edition 2021

DEDICATION

I'd like to NOT dedicate this book to BTS (the kpop boy band) and I DONT dedicate this book to whoever let me do that in my last book.

I dedicate this to those who support me online and in the real world.

I dedicate this to myself, and hope that soon I can travel again so I can "market" my book by reading it in airports like I did with my first book.

I most importantly dedicate this book to the love of my life, my Sun, Dale.

PREFACE

Magical yet mundane micro fiction stories/poems are one of my favourite things to write. Probably birthed from my love of Studio Ghibli films! I adore people, and the human condition is something that has interested me alot as I've grown up!

Oh, Insomnia!

Oh dried out flowers on the dining room table,
how you still smell so alive!
Fragrant perfume that smells like my late
Grandmother!

Oh mother, who cries out
"I haven't fed you yet!" As she hurries from the
bathroom, hair rollers still in her hair, to reach
up with her sore arm for Luna's cat biscuits!

Luna crunches on her bickies and I yawn.
I taste the lavender in the air, Luna continues to
crunch, and the birds chirp and sing back and
forth in a battle of the band's style - I am far too
exhausted to enjoy their concert.
But excited to get into this road trip because it
guarantees me at least an hour of sleep.

Gazing

I like to think of myself as the stars, sometimes.
My spine is a constellation, made up of immortal
stars; dying only to revive and then die once
more.

I look down on myself on Earth,
The starry night skyline acts as a mirror.
I look back up to myself, sitting on the grass.
For once the sky doesn't seem so daunting.
It's still endless, but instead of feeling this dread
- I can look up into the stars and ask my
boyfriend if he knows any constellations.

He spots a broken formation of stars, and jokes
that those stars are my spine and I reply
"So you're saying I'm a star"
We look into each other's eyes for a moment...
and just
laugh!

Van gogh Didn't Eat Yellow Paint To Be Happy

I thought if I bathed in yellow paint I could be
happy;
soak into my skin and turn me deranged,
convince myself that that this madness is true
bliss!

I thought happiness laid in the center of
sunflowers to be gently kissed by the sun!

Oh! To be a sunflower!
Oh! To be the sun!
Oh! To be happy!

Sometimes I think if you think about being
happy too much, it's impossible to be it.
It's something that lays in your center, to be
kissed gently by your sun's rays.

"You seem brighter" my mum said pulling me
into a hug when I moved out.

Sometimes, the sun's rays hide behind this dark mountain and you can't feel it's warmth on your rough, rocky surface.
You're not sure if it's even there. But other's can see it, and they'll point:
"Look! Over the horizon!"
And a new day starts.

A Phoenix Lives In My Pantry!

"My life is just one, big circle of failure!" my boyfriend cried as he tried to throw his stuff in the bin.
"I'm going round, and round! Nothing changes! It just goes back to the start!"
I sat on my mattress in the living room; our temporary couch.
In between hyperventilating I cried out that it didn't need to be.

The things that people said about you, didn't have to be true and things didn't have to go back to nothing if you tried. If you really, really tried and didn't expect things to fall apart immediately.

The bananas on the kitchen counter rotted, as we cried at each other back and forth, crunching on eggshells I didn't want to walk on anymore because I know throwing yourself away isn't a hint at suicidal thought!

It's just a step into the right direction towards
finally telling me what's on your mind! even if it
might upset me to hear that you're not sure if this
life is really that; a life.

You look at the bananas we haven't touched
since we bought them;
it's just another small thing for you to get
frustrated about;
like how we can't find a couch we like, there's
no stools for our breakfast bar - things aren't
happening as quick as we'd like and so in your
mind the world is ending! The world is ending!
So I'll save it!
There were stools sitting at the breakfast bar
when you came home from work.
And banana bread baking in the oven and our
couch will be in the lounge room if you'll just
come for a drive with me.

The Ocean Wants
To Go Home

I used to go to the beach at night, and I'd sit in
the cool sand to calm my soul and watch the
waves crash.

Sometimes, the waves would get so big and then
immediately fall;
as if the Ocean was reaching for someone and
she couldn't quite reach - even on her tippiest
toppiest toes and fell.

She tried all the time, with all her might towards
the stars.
To just reach out, and have no one answer her
back.

I couldn't help but imagine that when the Earth
was pretty much nothing, they really needed
someone.
And the Ocean? She was once a star that he fell
in love with.

She had a lover, who the Earth was very jealous of.
He'd always call to her, and she'd always tease him by dancing with her lover on the edge of the night sky.
But one night...
... she danced too close to the edge, and she fell to the Earth - who turned her into the Ocean so she could never return.

Sunday Lunch At Nunna's

I cannot help but feel a bit yellow over my
Nunna moving on.
To watch someone deteriorate for so long - that
last breath must have been so freeing! (Thats
how I like to think of it, at least. It keeps the
blues away)

I cannot help but feel a bit yellow over my
Nunna moving on.
Ever since my Grandmother left us, Nunna
would always ask for her.
She was trapped in this time loop; always
forgetting she was gone.

It tickles me pink to think that they're together
again.
They're both vibrant and young and it's like
they'd never lost eachother at all.

Maybe she's sitting on a bench up in those fluffy
clouds, in the arms of her husband.
Finally reunited after so long apart.

She's telling him all about the big family they
had created, how she'd missed him all of this
time and she cannot wait til she can see
everyone again, when we all come up for
Sunday lunch as the sun sets below.

Thinking like that keeps the deepest of blues far
away.

Good Soup

I find myself gurgling down the bath tub drain,
along with
the "purple rain" bath bomb water as I stayed in
for so long pieces of me fell away.

I sang to the scummy tiled walls until I became
a steamy. soupy mess - I forgot to leave I think.

Why Willow (Trees) Cry

Willow Trees make me think of grief stricken
women, slumped over crying.
I think back to times where Giants may have
roamed the Earth, dancing free, their long hair
dressed in flower petals, flowing in the wind.

One of the Giant women fell deeply in love with
a Human woman who had to go fight in the war
- to fight for her right to love.
It seems to never end.
She never returns.

Under the cover of night, the Giant woman will
go to her lover's grave, and weep for their
forbidden love.

Her grief is so heavy, she can't lift her body.
The grass grows over her legs - deeply rooted in
this grief.

Over time, the flowers weaved in her hair grew
to be leaves and throughout the years, she
became a Willow Tree.

Where Were You When The World Ended?

"Where were you when the world ended?"
In water that burned at the touch,
steam loosening up my clenched chest.
The scent of lavender unfurls me;
as if a flower, slowly blooming.

Sliding deep, deep, deeper into the tub
of relaxing lava - sighs of relief.

My tight body slowly, slowly releasing -
lightly floating amongst the starry petals
of the milky way.
Sliding deep into space;
but I do not scream,
I merely sigh with relief.

Dying Bouquet

I wonder if this is how the bouquet of flowers
my friend bought me for my birthday felt.
Crying out for their roots.
Beautifully, slowly, dying.
Only I don't find myself very beautiful.
Which is normally fine.
It's normally so fine, and I don't mind.
I just sing loudly when it rains in my bathroom, I
can't hear myself over the suds in my ears as I
wash my hair.
Pieces, falling away.
Always falling away.
Like this body,
Crying out for its roots.

Lavander Loves The Sun

His hand is the Sun!
And my waist is the pot of lavender that sits on
the window sill of my body!
When he rolls over in his sleep, it's like the
clouds interrupt a sun bathing cat;
Almost like when the hot water runs cold.

How could such a small touch give me such a
high?
I remember being in my early twenties, broken
hearted over a boy who told me he was like a
drug - but I disagree.
He was nothing.
Maybe a pain killer that I liked a bit too much
when I had my wisdom teeth pulled.

But this sunshine?
Those earthy eyes?
Rose petal lips?
Ocean soul?
Are something else!

A Conversation I Wish I Got To Have With My Dying Grandmother

Based on dialogue in the Midnight Gospel, episode 8: Mouse of Silver

Sitting beside her in her hospital bed,
The world ending just outside her window.
Gravity escapes the room, we both float, talking
as though we didn't notice.
Nothing else matters.
Maybe I'd talk about the things I like to do, to
avoid coming to terms with my Ninney dying.
Maybe she'd tell me that it's good to stay
present.
That we close our hearts to stay safe from the
idea that we, and everyone we love are going to
die.
My tears bubble and drift round the room and
my Ninney brings her hand to my cheek and
says

"and this? This opens them".

A gust of wind blows in and we drift away, into
this space dust.
A star twinkles and grows bright in the middle
of my misty body, Ninney's star dimming in hers
as we float through space.

The hospital crumbles away.
We don't notice.

"Opening your heart sucks" I cry.
"It hurts, yes".
"Will it always hurt?" My star bleeds brighter.
Ninney grabs it and holds it in our hands and it
forms into a sunflower.

"No it doesn't always hurt, but when it cracks
open, it really does. And when you lean into it...
It changes... And you know that what you're
experiencing is love, and it's the real deal!"
The sunflower explodes.
And propels us further into space, closer to a
black hole.
We don't notice.
But Ninney's mist begins to thin and distort -
leaving her barley recognisable.
"Well I love you very much, obviously"
I sniffle as we get closer to the black hole.

Only Ninney actually enters, and as she floats
away she'll say
"I love you too... And Chloe? That kind of love
isn't going anywhere. That's another thing you
may find. That I may leave this earth, sooner
rather than later but the love isn't going
anywhere"

The Window And The Sea

I like to watch the little fairies who live in a sea
glass house on the beach.
One night, a mermaid with starlight hair washes
up on the sand, tangled in a fisherman's net.
She wails in pain.
The fairies come to her aide.

One wants to help.
The Other insists she's an evil Siren and wants to
put her out of her misery.
They fight, and One takes a piece of sea glass
and cuts the net away from her.
The Other goes home in a huff.

The mermaid is thankful to the helpful fairy and
they form a friendship.
The Other fairy is so riddled with jealousy that
one night, as the mermaid slept, her starlight
flowing in the gentle lull of the sea slits her
throat with a piece of coral.

Her blood dyes her hair red and the lull returns
her to the sea.
One tearfully searches for their friend.
And I don't say anything.
I just close the window, and pretend it's wails are
the waves crashing on the beach.
I don't want to be next.

Bedside Friend

In my bedside draw lives a Dragon.
He loves not gold, but the trash that lives in my
drawers.
This little guy is the size of a rose petal, he even
uses the fake rose petals from an ex boyfriend as
bedding.
He is a turquoise color and he loves Easter
because that's when I fill the top draw with tiny
balls of foil from mini Easter eggs I like to binge
on in the night.

He loves not gold, but torn up pages from my
diary, and my passport.
He guards my birth certificate and the old
positive pregnancy tests that I can't bring myself
to throw away.

This little friend feasts on the bugs that live
amongst his treasure, as well as the crumbs from
chip packets I leave in there when I'm too lazy to
go to the bin.

He calls the beside table home, and I'll let him
stay there for as long as he doesn't burn me in
my sleep.

Thief!

Her backpack was stolen from her kitchen
counter.

She can't help but feel lost.
It had important cards,
Her parents address,
A negative pregnancy test,
But also much more.

It had little specs of sand from Lake Loch
Lamond and a faded ticket stub from the London
Eye, deep in the pockets.
A pin from the Louvre gift shop,
A wrapper from the first thing she ate in Japan.
The left strap was worn thin - she lived in this
thing as if it were a shell on her little hermit crab
back and now... It's just...
Gone.

How Did The Sky Look?

I used to want to swim in the clouds.
I thought it'd be like a giant bubble bath.
The birds could be my rubber duckies; the
planets my bath bombs.
I've always wanted to bathe in the Milky Way,
float in galaxies.

I want to bathe in water as hot as the Sun!
P e e l my skin off with a comet loofah - I want
my skin to be as smooth as I think Venus would
be if I could just
Touch it.
If I could just get up there...
To the sky that is.

Wings Made From Strings

I remember all the nights we'd sit in the park.
You told me that you wished you could fly, and
stepped closer to the edge of the playground.
I embroidered you some wings with my tears,
begging you to at least have a safe flight.
Take my hand, we'll walk down these stairs and
we can practice on the swings. As I make
sturdier wings, I'll push you as high as you
would like.
I will send you to share a kiss with the Moon!
And the stars! And whatever else it is you
believe in!

Please! Take your time for the come down,
there's no more flight once you go splat on the
concrete.
There is only the fall, into never ending night.

Enya And I

I found a note in my phone.
It was to remind myself what I wanted to talk
about with my psychologist.
So I must have wrote it some time ago - it's been
a while since she had time for me, and I don't
click with anyone else.

It read: my friendship circle isn't even a circle.
It's just a dot. It's a dot that disappears unless I
speak to it. It's all one sided. I am so sad.

I want to cry for that version of myself.
To be confined to such a loneliness.
To rather wallow in it.
Just incase the dot notices me, rather than truly
be on my own.

So desperate to be liked, it was as if I was
running to be the Mayor of Nothing.
Nothing but that dot.

But, I met a woman who I swear cries glitter,
and she is excited to be my friend. It makes me
feel so young.

Like I'm back in primary school where my best
friend drew me pictures of us as Sailor Moon
"just cos"!

I swear the gentle afternoon sun lives in her
laughter!
I feel wanted, and I want nothing more than to
gift her whatever I can find "just cos"!

Just because she seems to care that I exist.
Just because she seems as dorky as I am.
Just because she's gentle, kind and fierce all in
the same mighty breath!
Just because she exists, and I don't feel sorry for
existing at the same time as her.

Sunny Side Birthday

Dedicated to the due date that never came

I wonder what it would have felt like...
... Welcoming you into this world.
I'd have probably cried tsunamis!
But my storms would have calmed when I heard you.

I wonder if you'd have been swaddled in pink, or blue.
I like to think pink.
I'd always wanted a daughter.

I like to think you'd have my spiky hair,
probably black like your dad's.
You'd have my chubby chubby cheeks.
And you'd be perfect.
And small.
And ours.
And here.

I'd have so many booties crocheted for you as I waited for you to come Earth side.
I like to think that instead you're sunny side up, my lil eggy!
You'll probably meet your great grandmother, I do think she's there too after all.
I think she'd be spoiling you, and giving you all the love that I could not.

Lessons From Check Out #2

When I still worked at Woolworths,
I got a bit overexcited about how well
everything fit together, and made the bags too
heavy.
I apologise and tell the woman in the crochet
dress if she liked I could make it lighter.
She smiled at me with this kindness I haven't felt
from a stranger in some time.
As she lifts the bags into the trolley she says
"you're fine. I am quite strong. You've got to be
if you want to shop on your own"